To: Esther + Walter

From: Your Mt Zion Baptist Church
Sunday School Dept.

All our Love + Prayers.

POST CARDS

OF HISTORIC BLOWING ROCK

BLOWING ROCK HISTORICAL SOCIETY, INC.

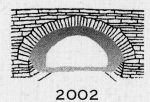

2002

PARKWAY PUBLISHERS, INC.
BOONE, NORTH CAROLINA

Available from:

Parkway Publishers, Inc.
P. O. Box 3678, Boone, North Carolina 28607
Telephone/Facsimile: (828) 265-3993
www.parkwaypublishers.com

Blowing Rock Historical Society, Inc.
P. O. Box 804
Blowing Rock, North Carolina 28605
Telephone: (828) 295-3021

Library of Congress Cataloging-in-Publication Data

Post cards of historic Blowing Rock / the Blowing Rock Historical Society, Inc.
    p. cm.
  ISBN 1-887905-54-5
      1. Blowing Rock (N.C.)--History--20th century--Pictorial works.
      2. Historic sites--North Carolina--Blowing Rock--Pictorial works.
      3. Postcards--North Carolina--Blowing Rock. I. Blowing Rock Historical Society.

F264.B59 P67 2001
975.6'843--dc21

2001053119

Typesetting and Editing: Julie Shissler
Cover Design, Book Design and Layout: Aaron Burleson, spokesmedia

The true building blocks of our village aren't brick and mortar, or even Grandfather stone and chestnut siding. The true building blocks are people; those who give Blowing Rock its incomparable grace, charm, and enchantment. It's Earl Trexler at the hardware, who will still fix your busted percolator; it's Ginny Stevens at the Historical Society, who gives us a vision for the future whether some of us want one or not; it's Jerry Burns who spreads his lovely generosity upon this little town like homemade apple butter on a biscuit. It's also the ones who came before us, who struggled up that high, green mountain by stagecoach, wagon, mule, and oxcart, to reach a place where, as the song says, "there's a cool wind shakin' th' stars around."

Over the years, which now number more than two hundred, a lot of personalities have rubbed off on Blowing Rock, giving it great variety, tender nuance, and good humor. What we find, however, whether we live here or come for a visit, is that Blowing Rock rubs off on us. And no matter how far we journey, or where our dreams take us, Blowing Rock has helped make us all who we are.

Here's our story, then, told in old post cards. Yet, it's the message written on the back of one card that tells our story best:

**"At last I am in God's country ...
I don't want to ever go home again."**

Jan Karon

Special Gifts

In memory of

Mary Bright by Banks C. Talley, Jr.

Jesse and Ethel Burns / Mr. and Mrs. W. L. Holshouser, Sr. by Jerry and Janice Burns

Mae Tester Coffey / Omer R. Coffey by Janice C. Herblin

The Daingerfield Family by Joe and Raleigh Dulaney

Rev. and Mrs. Frederick D. Frey by Bettie L. Frey

Rob and Nettie Greene / Emma Greene and Alma Miller by Caroline Greene Robbins

Helen and Shearon Harris by Jennie and Stuart Wallace

F. Gwyn and Mary Banks Harper by G. Alex Bernhardt, Sr. and Anne Harper Bernhardt

Dr. and Mrs. Walter K. Keys by Wat & Vania Keys

Bill and Lib Lentz / John and Bethsaide Lentz / George and Cora Sudderth by Barbara Lentz Wright

Mary C. Talley by Banks C. Talley, Jr.

Bill Williams by Julia Keys Williams

In honor of

All those who came before us who worked so hard to make our village the exceptional place that it is today.

THE BLOWING ROCK HISTORICAL SOCIETY
WISHES TO THANK

THE ETHEL AND W. GEORGE KENNEDY FAMILY FOUNDATION/
DIETER, MORGAN AND KARYN KENNEDY HERTERICH

and our 100 patrons, for their generous support

Welborn & Patty Alexander
Krishna P. Aluri and Mary Reichel
Appalachian Ski Mountain /
    The Moretz Family
Victoria Rosemond Appell
Richard E. Arey
Adair Phifer Armfield
Barbara & George Ball
Homer & Marge Barrett
Carolyn G. Baucom
Barbara Baker Beahn
John & Josephine Beall
Mr. & Mrs. David W. Beatty, Jr.
Lena R. & Paul A. Brooks
Henry & Dorothy Buchanan
Mr. & Mrs. Michael J. Cade
Mrs. Grace R. Carr
Chetola Mountain Resort
The Joe Clawson Family
Janice Greene Crumpler
Lila DeBow
Ann & Bill Dodge
Polly Dunne
Gwendolyn B. Dwyer
Meg & Frank Fary
Dorcas C. & Watson R. Gabriel, Sr.
William A. Gibbons
Robert B. & Peggy W. Gibson
Susie & Ann Greene
Dr. & Mrs. Max Gregory

Jack Dolliver & Ida Sanders Hall
Maurice R. & Mae Harrison
Mrs. Robert G. Hayes
Marge & Doug Hazen
Morgan & Jack Horner
Jan Karon
Rita Marotti Keramidas
Dr. Richard W. & Louann H. Kitchell
Mark & Betsy Klein
Col. William F. Koerschner
Opal B. Koone
Mayor J. B. & Lynn Lawrence
David & Linda Lehrman
Terry, Teresa, Tara & Tracy Lentz
Mr. & Mrs. Joe Lineberger
Jewell W. Loring
Irma Baker Lyons
T. Bragg McLeod
Sharon & John McNeely
Stuart & Carole Miller
Gordon & Malinda Mortin
Jeff & Catherine Norris
Louise & Ron Oberle
Parkway Café /
    Mr. & Mrs. Charles Hardin
Douglas L. Pegram
Judy H. Petrie
Mr. & Mrs. Edward W. Phifer III
Mary Adair E. Phifer
Al & Carol Rapp

Gwen C. Ratterree
Barbara Jordan & David Rawley
Mr. & Mrs. Hatton B. Rogers
Dr. & Mrs. Rion M. Rutledge
Arthur W. Singleton
Becky & Loyd Smith
Kay & Jim Snow
Mr. & Mrs. George C. Snyder, Jr.
J. Luther Snyder, II
Carole Spainhour
Ginny & Dave Stevens
Joyce & Jim Stines
Samuel Tallman & Michael Zuravel
Sylvia & Cullie Tarleton
Sue & Earl Taylor
Frank & Annie Hellen Thomas
Lowell & Ineke Thomas
Wes & Burr Thompson
Richard Trexler
Mr. & Mrs. Charles R. Vance, III
Virginia Vanstory
Ed & Tacky Vosburgh
Lillie & Henry Weathers
Al & Patty Wheeler
Gene & Lloyd Williams
Rita M. Wiseman
James G. Woolery
David Wray
Tucker & Ginny Yates
Lois M. Young

Acknowledgement

To the following who so generously shared their post cards so that this book could capture the best of the many post card collections of Blowing Rock's history. Our grateful thanks for coming forward and offering your cards for this book.

Reba and Grady Moretz/Appalachian Ski Mountain

The Blowing Rock Assembly Grounds

The Blowing Rock Pictorial History Museum

Mrs. John K. Barrow

Carrie and Robert Beard

Jerry W. Burns

Chetola Lodge & Conference Center

Toni Lentz Coffey

Stella Keller Dobbins

Raleigh and Joe Dulaney

Mary Lane Early

Nancy and Courtney Egerton

Francis (Pug) Greene

Jack M. Hall

David E. Harwood

Lynn S. Hill

Lynn and J.B. Lawrence

Nan and Edgar Lawton

Ralph E. Lentz II

Doug Marion

Mabel T. McLean

Sharon & John McNeely

Margaret H. Mordecai

Jeff and Catherine Norris

Judy H. Petrie

Clarence L. Pugh

Ginny A. Stevens

Louise W. Talley

Sylvia and Cullie Tarleton

Richard Trexler

June Herring Turner

Tacky and Ed Vosburgh

Nancy and Dick Vogt

Pam and Doug Washer

David Wray

Barbara Lentz Wright

Lois M. Young

Lawrence P. Zachary

BLOWING ROCK HISTORICAL SOCIETY, INC.
POST OFFICE BOX 804
BLOWING ROCK, NORTH CAROLINA 28605

September 2001

The members of the Blowing Rock Historical Society hope that you will enjoy this picture post card review of the unique assets of Blowing Rock, North Carolina.

The Society was formed in 1985 to protect and preserve historic resources important to the heritage of the town. It sponsors educational meetings and field trips, promotes the preservation of historic structures, operates a town museum, raises funds to finance its operations, and champions the conservation of natural resources.

Motivating the publication of this book was the desire to provide the reader with enlightenment about the town's historic resources and a feeling for that which precedes current memory. A celebration of what the Blowing Rock area has to offer -- both historically and scenically -- as well as a sense of the atmosphere and warmth of the village is captured in the book. This book is a scrapbook of what the town means to its residents as well as an advocacy for the protection of Blowing Rock's historic resources through a look into its past.

Special thanks for support of the project goes to two groups: the many persons, members of the Society and others, who shared post cards for use in the publication, and those patrons who, through their financial support, underwrote the costs of the project.

The proceeds of the project will be used for current Society projects such as hiring a consultant to prepare a nomination for Main Street as a National Register Historic District, creating a building fund to expand the museum and office space of the Society, augmenting the Society's endowment funds, and increasing the plaque program for historic sites and awards.

We appreciate your interest in this project. Welcome to historic, scenic Blowing Rock, and happy viewing!

Jeff L. Norris
President, 1999-2001

Barbara Lentz Wright
President, 2001-2003

The Post Card Book Committee:

Rao Aluri
Jerry W. Burns
Jack M. Hall
Richard Trexler
Ginny A. Stevens
Barbara Lentz Wright

The Blowing Rock Historical Society, Inc.
P. O. Box 804
Blowing Rock, North Carolina 28605

Table of Contents

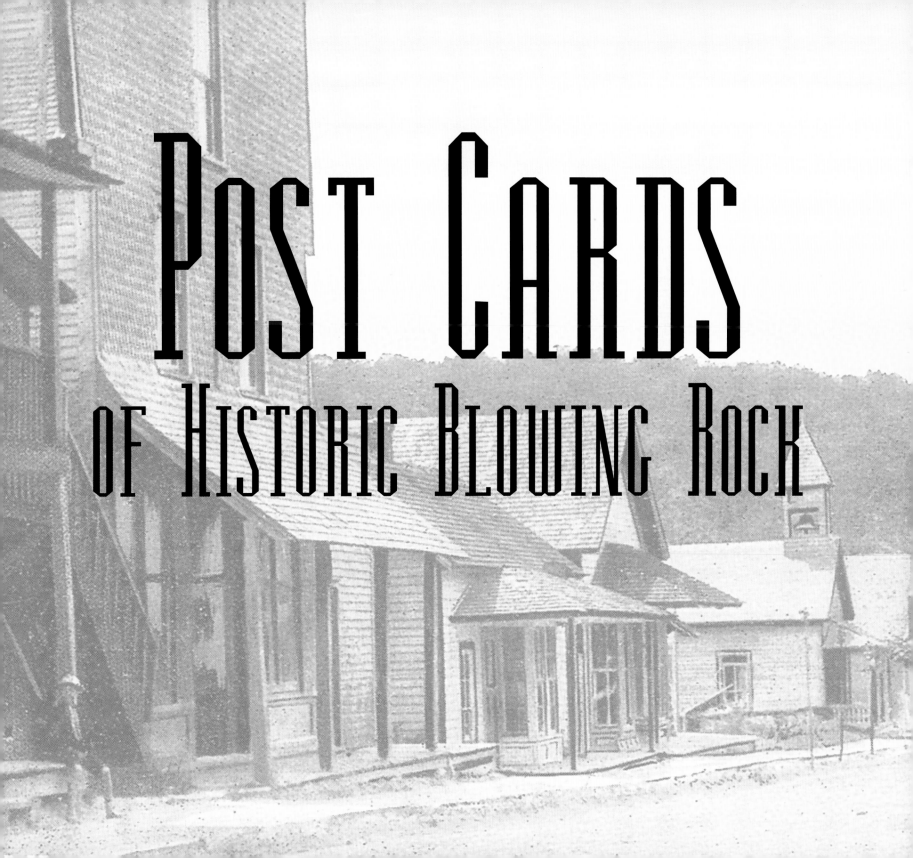

POST CARDS
OF HISTORIC BLOWING ROCK

Downtown and Main Street

Main Street, Blowing Rock, N. C.

On March 11, 1889, Blowing Rock was chartered and incorporated, with "Uncle Joe" Clarke serving as its very first mayor. Benjamin Harrison had just succeeded Grover Cleveland as President of the United States and Governor D. G. Fowle of Wake County had just been elected Governor of North Carolina. Blowing Rock, like so many other settlements throughout the land during the mid-1800's, was a beehive of activity. With a modest population of less than one hundred, it was eager to let the rest of the world know that its residents lived in the most beautiful place on earth. What better way to deliver that message than to use the new post card to share the vistas of the town and its magnificent setting?

693 LOOKING DOWN ON MAIN STREET, BLOWING ROCK, N. C.

Looking south down **Main Street**, *the stone building on the left is the Lentz Building. It was a filling station, an apartment building, the first bus station, a hardware store, and a clothing store. It has been expanded and now contains a number of shops.*

The little **Blowing Rock Pictorial History Museum** is now housed in the last surviving two-room rental cottage of the Watauga Hotel. In 1888 this cottage rented for $15 a month for room and board. It is located between the Martin House and the town's Memorial Park on Main Street. The town owns the building and the Blowing Rock Historical Society operates the Museum. This photograph was probably taken in the heavy snow of 1960.

The original **Episcopal Church and Reading Room**, with its distinctive bell tower, stood about where Sonny's Grill is now. It was the only public library for about ten years beginning in 1902. This building was destroyed in a 1923 fire, and according to legend, the bell tower was the last part of the structure to fall.

Public Library and Reading Room, Blowing Rock, N. C.

Street Scene - Blowing Rock, N.C.   1-B-96

Built into the stone facade of the **Parkway Hotel**, Blowing Rock's first geodetic survey benchmark gives, in 1933, the official elevation at 3,579. The U.S. Post Office was once housed in this building.

This card depicts a very early view of **Blowing Rock**. Even before its incorporation in March 11, 1889, Blowing Rock was a popular resort community for people seeking relief from the summer heat of the lower elevations.

Bird's Eye View of Blowing Rock, N. C. (Altitude 4030 feet)

Another early view of **Blowing Rock Main Street**, looking south. The two-story house on the left is the old Holshouser house, which was built at the end of the 19th century. It was located beside the present First Union National Bank.

Village of Blowing Rock, N. C. Altitude 4090 ft.

307:—U. S. Post Office, Blowing Rock, N. C. Elevation highest of any

P. O. East of the Rocky Mts. (Alt. 4090 feet).

25304

Before this one story building housed the **Parkway Hotel**, it was the Blowing Rock Post Office. The building was constructed circa 1924 of river and field rock. It now is home to Mountain View Realty and Main Street Gallery. This photo was taken around 1950.

The Vagabond Shop sold antique treasures and unique gifts at the intersection of Main and Maple Streets. Originally, this building served as Blowing Rock's first Town Hall and Chamber of Commerce. Built in the early 1900's, it now houses a gift shop, "Follow Your Dream."

Lamp Post Antiques sold English antiques and accessories on Main Street (at Pine Street) to townspeople and visitors. Built about 1887, the house once belonged to Colonel and Mrs. Ogden Edwards of Alabama, and today features foyer walls with a hand painted mural of the town. For years, Blowing Rock Realty has made its home in this historic house.

The advertisement on this card reads, "Main St., the Show Place of the Carolinas." Originally opened in a small Main Street building that currently houses Kohler's Real Estate, the **Blowing Rock Art Galleries** built a larger facility shown here. Auctions were held in the mornings and evenings, often drawing capacity crowds that spilled out onto the sidewalk.

Blowing Rock Art Galleries, located on Main Street across from Town Hall and Memorial Park, was operated for many years by the Mattar family. Old World Galleries is now located here.

Located across from the Martin House, *Fincke Gallery* was a popular auction for a number of years. The Gallery auctioned items from those valued at a few dollars to diamond jewelry, silver, rugs, and antiques. It is now the home of Kilwin's Chocolates and Ice Cream.

The **Blowing Rock Hospital** was erected in 1952 on Chestnut Drive, with Dr. Charles Davant, Jr. as its medical director. Health services were provided in a number of places in Blowing Rock until then, including Wallingford Clinic on Chestnut Street and Dr. Mary Warfield's clinic on South Main Street. The hospital has been expanded many times, but Dr. Charlie is still its shining star. The hospital is known as the Blowing Rock Hospital and The Charles Davant, Jr. Extended Care Facility.

Pictured here in these late-1940 cards is the home built for James Milton and his wife, Abbie Rockefeller, in 1932 by Lloyd Robbins. It was purchased later by Mrs. Julius Cone (Laura), who was a relative of the Moses Cone family. She lived there until the late 1960's and entertained many of the Cone family members, including Etta, in this living room. This home, which sits on the John's River Gorge and contains furniture made locally by the Moodys and Whites, is now a private residence.

THE BLOWING ROCK

The **Blowing Rock** continues to be a symbolic promontory for visitors.
The Town of Blowing Rock takes its name from The Rock. Native
Americans were the first to marvel at The Rock and the scenery.

Blowing Rock, Blowing Rock, N. C.

1912

Blowing Rock;
Grandfather Mountain in Distance.
Blowing Rock, N. C.

The profile of Grandfather Mountain is visible in this view across from the Johns River Gorge as seen from The Rock.

This hand-colored card of the **Blowing Rock**, one of the earliest cards produced, was postmarked June 11, 1912.

GREETINGS FROM

THE ROCK
BLOWING ROCK, N.C.

BLOWING ROCK

GRANDFATHER M.T.
SEEN FROM
BLOWING ROCK, N.C.

in
NORTH
CAROLINA

ENTRANCE TO THE ROCK
BLOWING ROCK
N.C.

13

Magnificent sunset at **Blowing Rock** *showing Grandfather Mountain and the scenic Blue Ridge Mountain range beyond.*

110:—Sunset view at Blowing Rock, Grandfather Mt. in Right, Western North Carolina.

22223

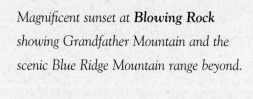

N-748   MOONLIGHT SCENE OF BLOWING ROCK, N. C.

E.7871

ALTITUDE 4,350 FEET...-"IN THE LAND OF THE SKY"

This hand-colored card has been made to look like nightfall. The caption on the back says: "From Blowing Rock can be seen a far-flung panorama of magnificent mountain scenery that is unsurpassed. This colossal rock, leaning over the deep dimensions of John's River Gorge, derives its name from the fact that at nearly all times a strong wind is blowing at this point. Here wind currents defy the laws of nature, and it is said that if a light object, such as a handkerchief, or a straw hat, is thrown from The Rock, it will be blown back by the force of the wind sweeping up from the gorge below -- 'Believe it or not'!"

48:– BLOWING ROCK, ALTITUDE 4350 FEET, WESTERN NORTH CAROLINA.

BLOWING ROCK, BLOWING ROCK, N. C.   B-94

The **Blowing Rock** has been photographed over the years from many angles and perspectives. "The Rock" was featured in the 1940's in Ripley's "Believe It or Not" column as "the place where it snowed upside down".

304—Blowing Rock, Alt. 4000 Ft. and the Rock Tavern, Western North Carolina

9A-H2484

These two cards
show **The Rock**
and the ***Gift Shop***.
The card at the top
is a hand-colored,
and the lower one
is a photograph.

The Rock Tavern
At The Blowing Rock
Blowing Rock, N. C.

9941

The **Rock Tavern**, *a grill in the 1930's, is now a rustic gift shop, as well as the entrance to the Blowing Rock viewing area.*

INTERIOR, ROCK TAVERN, BLOWING ROCK, N.C.

This was an interior view of the gift area at the **Rock Tavern**, along with a view of the exterior, featuring exquisite native rock-work, and the view of "never-never-land".

THE ROCK TAVERN
BLOWING ROCK, N.C.

18

*This is an early card of the observation tower before the **Rock Tavern** was built. Snacks, drinks and souvenirs were sold here to the visitors.*

*This is the first observatory built after the **Rock Tavern**. It was equipped with a long distance viewing device that helped pinpoint special vistas.*

*At the turn of the 20th century, these well-dressed tourists enjoy the view from **The Rock** and write home to tell of their adventure in Blowing Rock.*

19

Observation Point

N-623   BLOWING ROCK—LENOIR HIGHWAY AS SEEN FROM BLOWING ROCK OBSERVATORY.

WESTERN NORTH CAROLINA

Photo by Emerson Humphrey

E-5765

*These two cards show the **observatory** after it was enlarged. The Lenoir Turnpike (now US 321) is in the lower portion of this 1950's card.*

It is hard to read, but this card may say "Asa Barringer" in the sign on the car, suggesting it belonged to Osmond Barringer of Charlotte, who brought the first automobile to Blowing Rock on September 20, 1908. The new "horseless carriage" could climb anything!

America's Switzerland.
The unrivalled Blowing Rock Country.
The famous "Blowing Rock"
(altitude 4090 feet)
near Blowing Rock, N. C.

There was a time that one could drive right up to **The Rock** as seen in these two early post cards.

Near View of Blowing Rock, N.C.

This hand-colored card from shortly after
the turn of the century recalls the romantic
moonlit mountain views.

118:—Moonlight on the Johns River Valley and Blowing Rock, Western North Carolina.

22231

1936

America's Switzerland. The Unrivalled Blowing
Rock Country. The Famous Blowing Rock,
Altitude 4300 ft. Blowing Rock, N. C.

One more reference to **Blowing Rock**
as "America's Switzerland" in this old
post card, in circulation around 1927.
To this day, there is no clear consensus
on Blowing Rock's altitude, but this
card puts it at 4,300 feet.

According to Native American legend, light objects can be blown back up after being thrown from **The Rock**.

N-789   MID-WINTER AT BLOWING ROCK, WESTERN NORTH CAROLINA

E-9461

These folks seem to have a bit more nerve than most of us today, standing on the snow-covered **Rock**, waiting for the wind to whip up from the Johns River Gorge.

On top of Blowing Rock, Altitude 4250 feet
Blowing Rock, N. C.

Blowing Rock

People on **The Rock** have long been a favorite subject for post cards. Clothing helps us date the cards. Notice how the altitude of our town's namesake seems to change from card to card!

CHURCHES

Churches are a major component of Blowing Rock's community structure. We celebrate the buildings, the gardens and people who have made them a vital part of living in this village.

This beautiful bronze is the focal point for the Mary Garden at **St. Mary of the Hills Episcopal Church**. *It was sculpted by the late Marjorie Daingerfield Lundean, daughter of internationally known artist Elliott Daingerfield, who maintained his studio at Westglow in Blowing Rock.*

Mount Bethel Reformed Church, known as "the Little White Church by the side of the road", is Blowing Rock's oldest church edifice, built in 1882. The cemeteries in front and behind the church contain the town's first known grave and tombstone from 1794. The Church is now under the care of The Blowing Rock Assembly Grounds.

Land was deeded in 1900 for **The Blowing Rock Methodist Church**. Built of native timber and stone, it was originally covered in chestnut bark, which was replaced by poplar bark in 1999. It is equipped with long, straight-backed benches and has a seating capacity of about 150. It is open seasonally for services.

"The Lord's House...in the top of the mountains."
—Isaiah 2:2

26

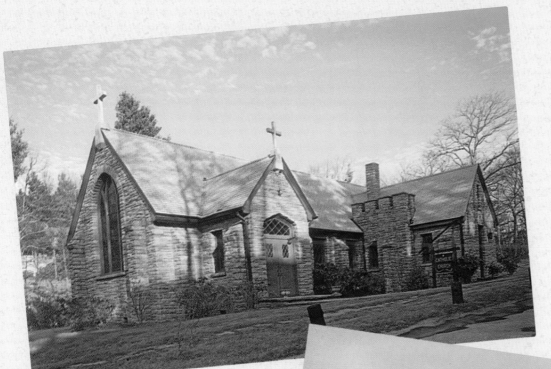

The Church of the Epiphany was constructed in 1948 on donated land at the edge of the Blowing Rock Golf Course. The congregation, however, has been in existence since 1933, when it held its services at Mayview Manor and the Yonahlossee Theater. It has served the Catholic community for over fifty years and is also open seasonally.

The **Christian Science Church** was built in 1955. Prior to its construction, the congregation held its services at various locations for over 20 years. The church has been open year-round since it was winterized in 1967. Its Christian Science Reading Room serves the community by making religious literature available to the public.

First Baptist Church *was organized in 1903.*
Its first sanctuary was erected in 1905 on Main
Street under a large maple tree, to which horses
were hitched during the services. A new building
was constructed on Sunset Drive in 1968 to
house the rapidly expanding congregation. The
"old" church building still stands, and has
housed a gift shop and restaurants.

BR-1   FIRST BAPTIST CHURCH, BLOWING ROCK, N. C.

Episcopal Church, Blowing Rock, N. C.

*The **Episcopal Church** may be the most photographed*
church in Blowing Rock. The worship services must have
begun in this simple little frame building whose location is
unknown. Next came the Episcopal Chapel and Reading
Room, built in 1890 with its distinctive bell tower. It stood
on Main Street where Sonny's Grill is now located, and
contained the town's only public library from 1902-1912.
The fire of 1923 consumed the church, as well as a
number of other buildings on the east side of the street.

The cornerstone of a new and larger Episcopal Church was laid in 1918 and construction completed in 1921. It was originally named **Stringfellow Memorial Church**.

104:—Stringfellow Memorial Episcopal Church, Blowing Rock, N. C.

STRINGFELLOW MEMORIAL CHURCH (EPISCOPAL), BLOWIN

W. W. Stringfellow, who owned Chetola, made a generous thank-offering to the church in gratitude for having missed sailing on the RMS Titanic. Mrs. Susie Stringfellow, his wife, died in 1920 and a memorial plaque was placed in the nave of the church.

Elliott Daingerfield donated his painting, **Madonna of the Hills**, shortly thereafter, and the church was renamed **St. Mary of the Hills Episcopal Church**. The magnificent maple tree, which has grown old with the church, is carefully protected.

12

Presbyterian Church, Blowing Rock, N. C.

The original **Rumple Memorial Presbyterian Church** was dedicated on July 26, 1886. The small frame church was severely damaged by lightning two years later. The larger stone building pictured here was completed in 1912. Note the gravestones in the side yard.

The **Rumple Memorial Presbyterian Church** underwent expansions and renovations over the years. The church is still a vibrant part of the Blowing Rock community. Note the changing entrance, which now contains an extraordinary stained glass window.

Shown to the right is one of Blowing Rock's oldest houses, built in the 1880's by Confederate Major Henry Franklin Schenck, an early cottager.

731   PRESBYTERIAN CHURCH, BLOWING ROCK, N. C.

4A7S

ESTATES

Cone's Mansion, near Blowing Rock, N. C.

Snyder Estate   Blowing Rock, N. C.

Two famous landmarks in Blowing Rock were identified by their familiar architecture. **Flat Top Manor**, the "summer home" of Bertha and Moses Cone, celebrated its centennial in 2001. This picture of the grand estate was on a post card in circulation only three years after the mansion was completed and occupied.

This is the **Snyder Estate,** as it was known in the 1940's. It has also been home to the Estes and Stringfellow families, and is now one of the High Country's most prestigious developments, Chetola Resort.

Few places in Western North Carolina can boast of both the natural and man-made beauty that makes landscapes special. One of those unique places is **Chetola**, a place that once was the seasonal home of one of the South's most famous families, and now is one of the High Country's most spectacular resort communities.

The scenes here depict the famed property as it appeared when it was a private residence. Reflecting in the stillness of graceful Silver Lake, as it was called in the early 1900's, the Chetola manor house is an architectural marvel, unique and distinctive to the mountains.

"CHETOLA" BLOWING ROCK, N. C.

103:— "Had-Er-Way" Formerly Chetola Estate, Blowing Rock, N. C.

Chetola, which in the Cherokee language means "Haven of Rest", once belonged to the Stringfellow family, which led the building of St. Mary of the Hills Episcopal Church. The Stringfellow family helped make the landmark church the home of one of Elliott Daingerfield's most famous paintings, "Madonna of the Hills."

Chetola was later acquired by the "Coca Cola King", Luther Snyder. It was the Snyder family which added a majority of the landscaping that makes Chetola so special.

One of the interesting things about Chetola is the many spellings of its name over the years. Post cards and other old photographs of the historic property have identified it as everything from "Chattolo" and "Cheeteela" to "Chestola", "Colola", and "Had-Er-Way" which has been cancelled out.

These three views of **Chetola** span a time frame of 1902 through 1975.

Through the ownership of the Stringfellows and Snyders, to the present day owners, this historic property has been a proud part of our community.

BR-3 "CHETOLA" THE SNYDER ESTATE, BLOWING ROCK, N. C.

Although **Chetola Estate** has always been a private property, it has belonged to the people of Blowing Rock because they have always been made welcome at this beautiful retreat in the heart of the village.

The Blowing Rock Country, "Chatola."

Parkway Craft Center on the Blue Ridge Parkway
Moses H. Cone Memorial Park near Blowing Rock, N. C.

The magnificent architecture of **Flat Top Manor** is surpassed only by Biltmore Estate in Asheville, and it is recognized as one of North Carolina's most famous historic private homes. Like Biltmore, the private home of the Vanderbilt family, Flat Top Manor was one family's dream of elegance in the mountains. Moses and Bertha Cone moved to Blowing Rock from Baltimore, and began developing their grand estate at the turn of the century. Moses Cone himself named his home "Flat Top Manor" after the mountain on which it was built.

In 2001 **Flat Top Manor** celebrated 100 years, having been completed in 1901 at a cost of around $75,000. With several lakes, miles of carriage and foot trails, acres of apple orchards, and a number of other historic outbuildings, the Cone Estate is the pride of the Blue Ridge Parkway; the Parkway actually meanders through the property.

Looking across the dam at **Bass Lake**, with Flat Top Manor barely visible at the left center, puts this grand mountain estate into a whole new perspective. In this view from a card dated 1909, it is evident that Mr. and Mrs. Cone had not finished their elaborate landscaping plans. Two things stand out in this old photograph. First, the small land mass that now makes up the Bass Lake island was once attached to the shoreline, creating a peninsula. Second, we notice signs at the lower right which show, even at this early stage of the development of their estate, the Cone family welcomed visitors and local residents to use the carriage and walking trails.

"Lake on Flat Top Manor Orchard Estate" Blowing Rock, N. C.

America's Switzerland. The unrivalled Blowing Rock Country.
Lake on Cone Estate. Blowing Rock, N. C.

These post cards capture the Manor as it appeared high on the hillside from Bass Lake. Today the Manor is home to the Southern Highland Handicraft Guild, and most of the Manor's first floor is open to the public. The Park Service also operates a Visitor Information Center at the Manor which provides numerous publications about its fascinating history.

105:—Nightime, The Cone Estate from Across the Lake, Blowing Rock, N. C.

22218

105

N-541   LAKE ON THE CONE ESTATE, BLOWIN

Cone Lake on Cone Estate, Blowing Rock, N. C.

E.5327

3,600 acres of the most beautiful part of the Blue Ridge Mountains is how some describe the **Cone Estate**. Known as "The Denim King", Moses Cone lived just long enough to see his Flat Top Manor finished. He was intent on making his new mountain retreat a producing farm.

With lakes, vegetable gardens, massive apple orchards, and cattle, his grand estate was for work and play. These three old photos, circa 1920's, show **Bass Lake**, the large body of water visible from the Manor's front entrance.

Acknowledged as one of America's great land-scape and portrait artists, **Elliott Daingerfield** selected Blowing Rock as his home.

Daingerfield's Mansion.
Blowing Rock, N. C.

It was from his impressive home here in the Blue Ridge that Daingerfield was inspired to do some of his most memorable works. The subject for his landscapes was provided right at the front entrance to his magnificent estate home. The gardens surrounding the main house provided the backdrop for many other works, from portraits to still lifes.

One of his most famous works, **Madonna of the Hills**, hangs in the main sanctuary of St. Mary of the Hills Episcopal Church on Blowing Rock's Main Street, a lasting tribute to this great American artist, who had a significant international impact in the early 1900's.

Elliott Daingerfield, Blowing Rock's most famous artist, painted these two post cards, and even stated in his own handwritten note attached to the cards: "Important...water color cards by Elliott Daingerfield." Born in Harper's Ferry, Virginia, (now West Virginia) on March 26, 1859, Daingerfield pursued his art career in New York City, and came to Blowing Rock in 1885 to recuperate from diphtheria. He fell in love with the North Carolina mountains and spent much of his time in Blowing Rock, building three homes: Edgewood Cottage, Windwood, and Westglow. He was noted as a religious painter, but he is also known for scenic portrayals of the southwest which were commissioned by the Santa Fe Railroad.

Called a "Victorian Visionary", Daingerfield was one of the most prominent impressionists of the late 19th century. He died in 1932 at the age of 73, but left a legacy of artistic excellence to this community and to the world.

Blowing Rock capitalized on the era of post-Victorian
romance to welcome visitors to its hotels and inns.

Martin Cottage, Blowing Rock, N. C.

MARTIN COTTAGE, BLOWING ROCK, N. C.

The Martin House, *built in 1870 as a private residence, became a boarding house to serve the summer visitors. Rooms were added to the house to accommodate fourteen guests. The Martins, whose reputation for hospitality was legendary, graciously provided exceptional food and entertainment. This card is dated June 26, 1934.*

The Martin Cottage *was advertised in 1942 as "'Not a hotel, but a Home' for summer guests on the crest of the Blue Ridge Mountains -- Elevation over 4000 feet - Open April to October."*

41

With improved communications in the 1880's, lowlanders became aware of the refreshing cool mountain air and magnificent vistas in Blowing Rock. Tourism flourished and the boarding houses could not meet the need for accommodations. To meet this increasing demand, the **Watauga Hotel** was built in 1888. It occupied most of the land where Memorial Park is now located. Room and board for the summer of 1888 was $15 a month. As the first of the larger hotels, it was overcome with seasonal visitors and soon added a series of cottages, of which the one surviving is now occupied by the Blowing Rock Museum. This Hotel was completely destroyed by fire in the early 1900's and was immediately rebuilt on the same foundation and renamed the Watauga Inn. The Inn was razed by fire in 1926 and the property remained unused until 1939 when the town purchased it for a park. This card is dated June 26, 1912.

In the 1920's, one of the area's favorite gathering places for ladies was the **Hob Nob Tea Room** on the north end of what is now Memorial Park/Town Hall property.

Watauga House, Blowing Rock, N. C.

HOB NOB Tea House, Blowing Rock, N. C.

The Watauga Inn - Blowing Rock, N.C.   1-8-86

In September 1928, the Hob Nob Inn, further north on Main Street from the park, was converted into a year-round hotel named the **New Watauga Inn**. It ended its successful operation in 1956 when flames engulfed the Inn. Never again has another building in Blowing Rock been named "Watauga".

The Watauga Inn - Blowing Rock, N.C.   1-B-86

BR-4 HIGHWOOD INN, BLOWING ROCK, N. C.

The **Highwood Inn**, owned and operated by Mr. and Mrs. J. K. Smith, advertised itself as "a modern guest home, located in the heart of the Blue Ridge Mountains, with twin beds, private baths and close to restaurants and shopping center." It is located on Morningside Drive and is now a private residence.

The Blowing Rock Hotel opened in spring 1889 to accommodate the burgeoning number of summer visitors. In 1889, the newly incorporated Village of Blowing Rock had 200 inhabitants in the winter and 600 in the summer. There were three hotels, the Watauga, Blowing Rock and Fairview, along with boarding houses such as the Bradys and Stuarts. The superb location at South Main Street and Chestnut Drive was a major drawing card for the hotel. The stone columns across the street from the hotel and next to the twig bench still remain at the entrance to a private home. This card is dated 1911.

Blowing Rock Hotel, Blowing Rock, N.C.

Pub. by W.C. Vannoy

9449. Blowing Rock Hotel, Blowing Rock, N. C.
Altitude 4250 ft.

The **Blowing Rock Hotel** reached the height of its popularity in the late 20's and early 30's, and celebrated its 50th anniversary in 1939, boasting that it was the oldest resort hotel in the United States owned and continuously operated by the same family. The hotel closed in the early 1940's. These cards are postmarked 1932.

127:—Blowing Rock Hotel, Blowing Rock, N. C.

22240
1932

This panoramic card was photographed by Earl Hardy, a noted photographer from Lenoir, North Carolina. Hardy photographed many Blowing Rock attractions in the 1920's to 1940's for cards which were published by the Asheville Post Card Company. Note the cottages, two of which still stand in their original location.

BLOWING ROCK HOTEL
ABOVE THE CLOUDS

BLOWING ROCK, N. C.
ELEVATION 43,00

SKYLAND INN, BLOWING ROCK, N. C.

The Skyland Inn, a private home converted to house seasonal guests, was one of the village's older establishments. It was built in 1891 by the Stuart family and closed in 1914. The Inn was also known as Stuart Hotel. E. J. Blackwell, a Florida businessman, purchased it in 1945. Its superb location on the ridge has a view that spanned a hundred miles and was one of the finest in the area.

In 1945 E.J. Blackwell bought the Stuart Hotel (originally the Skyland Inn) and changed its name to **The Farm House Inn** in 1951. The breathtaking views of the John's River Gorge and Grandfather Mountain enticed most visitors to spend several weeks there. Bluegrass music was played in the 40's and 50's but the music shifted to Broadway tunes when E.J., Jr. and Shirley Blackwell took it over in 1954. They recruited staff with musical abilities and the Farm House Singers became a hallmark for the restaurant, inn and the community.

The Farm House was closed in 1998. After about a year of fruitless efforts to save it, the Farm House was demolished in 1999 and the land was sold for private residences.

An aerial view in 1968 says that The **Green Park Hotel** was "a complete resort hotel overlooking the Blowing Rock Country Club and Golf Course." The lower card is the view from the Lenoir-Blowing Rock Turnpike (now US 321).

312—Green Park Hotel, Alt. 4,000 Ft., Blowing Rock, N. C.

© CURT TEICH & CO., INC.   5B-H160

Green Park Hotel.   Green Park, N. C.

The Green Park community, with its own post office, was separate from Blowing Rock until annexed by the town in November 1926. The heart of that community was **The Green Park Hotel**. Opened in 1891, it was operated not only as a hotel to visitors but also as a gathering spot for Green Park residents. This card, made in New York and hand-colored, predated the annexation of Green Park, North Carolina.

Note the casino to the left of this old card. In 1938 dances at the Green Park Casino were 50 cents per couple, except Saturdays, when it rose to 80 cents. In contrast, at Mayview, the dances were $1.25, thus giving the Green Park the reputation of being as comfortable and plain as an "old shoe." But it was also thought to be expensive, with dinner costing $2.50.

The Blowing Rock Country,
Green Park Hotel, Green Park, N. C.
Altitude 4300 Ft.

Pub. for Green Park Hotel.

Flowers have long been an important seasonal statement for Blowing Rock. We do not know when the **Green Park** first planted this descriptive garden on the hillside across the road (the Blowing Rock-Lenoir Turnpike, now US 321) from the hotel, but we know it delighted many for a period of years in the mid 1900's. The hillside was used for games and demonstration riding at the first horse show in Blowing Rock in 1923, before it was moved to the Tate Horse Show Grounds in Mayview. Even today, when we have had a rainy spring, and the meadow is closely mown, one can see where this garden was planted as "GREEN PARK HOTEL" is spelled out in the lush light green grass, where the water pools at the base of the excavations for the old letters, indicating where the garden had once been planted. Look for it, and smile at this special part of our history.

Headwaters of the Yadkin River are just South of the Green Park Hotel as noted in this card.

SCENE FROM THE HEAD SPRING OF THE YADKIN RIVER LOOKING TOWARD THE GREEN PARK HOTEL
GREEN PARK, N. C.

N-751   GREEN PARK HOTEL AND A FEW OF THE COTTAGES, BLOWING ROCK, N. C.

E-7874

*The **Green Park** cottages were favorite spots for families to stay. The hotel was noted for its informal and friendly atmosphere. The post card says, "Your vacation here will mean more in hours of recreating rest and more in rich and happy memories."*

*By 1913, the **Green Park** **Hotel** was "the place to stay" in the mountains, and many visitors spent the entire season there.*

Green Park Hotel Cottages
Green Park, N. C.

Green Park Hotel - Blowing Rock, N.C.

As the years changed the Grand Dame of Blowing Rock, the words of Mrs. Vickie Sylvia, who supervised twenty waitresses at the hotel in the early 1920's suggest the biggest change from current times; she notes that the waitresses made $12 per month and about a dollar a day in tips. They worked from 7 a.m. to 10 p.m. and took great pride in their service.

N-752   GREEN PARK HOTEL, BLOWING ROCK, N. C.

E-7875

429:—GREEN PARK HOTEL, BLOWING ROCK, N. C.

29198

Times have changed, but Blowing Rock is grateful that this special part of her history is still "alive and well" and we thank all who have cared for this old hotel during the past fifty years for sustaining this remarkable landmark.

The arrival of Walter L. Alexander in Blowing Rock in 1917 marked the beginning of the town's most dynamic and well-publicized development. Mr. Alexander transformed the land to the west of the village into a carefully planned and skillfully marketed development called Mayview Park. Blowing Rock was to become "America's Switzerland" and the climate, views, flora and fauna, and fine recreational activities of the area were touted while cottages and homes were planned for seasonal residents.

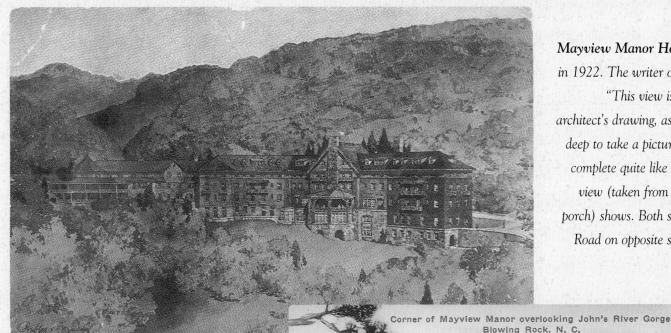

Mayview Manor Hotel was opened in 1922. The writer of this card said: "This view is made from the architect's drawing, as the gorge is too deep to take a picture from. It is not complete quite like this as the other view (taken from about our room porch) shows. Both southwest views. Road on opposite side of building."

Corner of Mayview Manor overlooking John's River Gorge. Blowing Rock, N. C.

This card, from a hand-colored photograph by Earl Hardy, shows the magnitude of the view across the gorge from the Manor. The card dates to 1930's era.

108:-MAYVIEW MANOR, BLOWING ROCK, NORTH CAROLINA

49918

The architecture of **Mayview Manor** was unparalleled in the High Country in the mid-1920's. Chestnut bark covered the exterior, while "clear" chestnut woodwork was featured on the interior. Porches and ornamentation used native timbers, and 16 chimneys capped native rock fireplaces.

129:-PARTIAL VIEW OF MAYVIEW MANOR, BLOWING ROCK, N. C.

22311

Model T's brought political celebrities, movie stars and convention guests to the cool mountains. Sharpshooter Annie Oakley managed the Gun Club at the Manor in 1924.

2A79

Entrance to Mayview Manor.   Blowing Rock, N. C.

The entrance to the hotel set the image for the elegance of style and first class service that became **Mayview Manor's** hallmark.

The 138-room structure had a unique style dubbed "Early Appalachian" and was beautifully appointed with comfortable, but not opulent, mountain furnishings. Thomas Broyhill and C.E. Hayworth purchased the hotel in 1927, selling a portion of it to Mr. Milton Chapman in 1930. Mr. Chapman, whose name was synonymous with fine hotels in Florida, brought the same high standard of service to Blowing Rock as owner/manager until 1966.

Section of Mayview Manor Lobby.   Blowing Rock, N. C.

Section of
Mayview Manor Dining Room
Blowing Rock, N. C.

During that long period the "pride of manor" was the endless supply of culinary delights, lovely floral arrangements, Horse Show breakfasts, Boots and Saddle Balls, bingo nights, theme dances, children's parties and daily events to keep the guests and townspeople in a social whirl. **Mayview Manor** was the "Queen" of Blowing Rock hotels.

Fine food, elegant entertainment
and extraordinary social occasions
and dances made this Ball Room a
lively part of the Manor almost
nightly. Known for a continual
array of events during the season,
Mayview Manor gave the best
that Blowing Rock could offer to
the seasonal visitors.

Section of Mayview Manor Ball Room.   Blowing Rock, N. C.

BR-5 Airplane View of Mayview Manor, Blowing Rock, N. C.

This aerial view shows the
tremendous size of the
Mayview Manor complex.
The Manor was closed in
1966, demolished in 1978,
and the land was sold for
development. The loss of
Mayview Manor was a low
point in our village's history.

"One cent for United States and Island Possessions, Cuba, Canada and Mexico. Two Cents for foreign."
This was truly a penny post card.

The **Appalachian Motel** advertised itself as "located on US 321-Blowing Rock Highway just off the Blue Ridge Parkway" as well as proclaiming it was an "in Resort Town, Blowing Rock, NC, and had excellent accommodations, bordering on a beautiful lake." Competition between motels was rigorous in the 1950's and the best advertising brought the highest number of tourists. This is now the Brookside Inn; the lake in front is shaped like a fish with the island being the eye.

The **Yonahlossee Motel's** advertising says that it was located on US 221 near the Blue Ridge Parkway. The copy on the back of the card indicated twenty well appointed guest rooms, and that it was located on North Main Street. This is now the Blowing Rock Inn. Note that Yonahlossee was spelled many different ways throughout the years, but this seems to be the spelling that stuck.

Atop one of the highest perches in the town, **Cliff Dweller Motel** is located on US 321 Bypass, one mile south of the Blue Ridge Parkway. The motel advertised its "beautiful view from each room". Now known as the Cliff Dwellers Inn, the view encompasses Chetola Resort, Shoppes on the Parkway, and the surrounding mountains.

Hillwinds Inn, located on Sunset Drive and Ransom Street, was opened in 1970. Its advertisement capitalized on the fact that it is only two blocks from the Village. A restaurant called the Pancake House was previously located on the property.

The **Hemlock Motel**, nestled in the hemlocks, was located on Morris Street. Its advertisement said that it was off "The Blue Ridge Parkway in the village off the highway." The motel is now the Homestead Inn. Note the brick building in the background, which was the Blowing Rock High School. During the 1960's Watauga school district was consolidated, and the Blowing Rock High School was replaced by Watauga High School in 1965. The Blowing Rock High School was torn down.

The Ranch Motel and Restaurant was another business to mention the popular Blue Ridge Parkway in its advertising, noting that it was located on the Parkway, one mile north of Blowing Rock, in "35 acres of quiet". The name has been changed to the New River Inn and Navelli's Restaurant.

Still owned by Glenn Coffey, the **Blue Ridge Court** later changed its name to the Blue Ridge Motel. Located on US Routes 221 and 321A (North Main Street) it was conveniently close to the village, and has the unique honor of having a rock monument denoting the Daniel Boone Trail on its property.

Blowing Rock Tourist Court used a popular term of the 1950's when tourist courts were located in homes, newly built motels and other appropriate buildings. It advertised that it was "one block off Main Street and had 12 modern units." This was one of the original motels in Blowing Rock, and became Blowing Rock Motor Court. It was recently demolished.

SOME OF THE COTTAGES AT RHODODENDRON MOTOR LODGE, BLOWING ROCK, N. C.

Rhododendron Motor Lodge *was another early guest facility, located on the Linville Road at Main Street, and offering "hotel rooms and cottages, with twelve accommodations and twelve baths at the altitude of 4,000 feet". It also advertised itself as "the quiet court in the village, two blocks to stores and movies. Open April 10 - November 1. Mr. and Mrs. Bertram Hildebrand, owners-managers." Currently the complex encompasses Cheeseburgers Grill and Paradise Bar, with small shops located in the cottages.*

Mountainaire Motor Court *was one of the many guest accommodations that featured the word "motor" in its name, capturing the resurgence of automobile travel after World War II's gas rationing ended, and families took to the road once again for their vacations. "Located on US 221/321 and the Blue Ridge Parkway" the court stated that it was a "new attractive 12 unit court" on North Main Street. It is now named Mountainaire Inn & Log Cabins.*

MOUNTAINAIRE MOTOR COURT, BLOWING ROCK, N.C.

E-13649

When the American Automobile Association began giving its approval to motels and hotels, its logo was used in advertising. The **Mount View Motel** proudly advertised its location on US 221/321 two miles north of the business district, and stated that it had "AAA lovely rooms with private balconies overlooking a small lake." It is now The Timber Lodge.

MOUNT VIEW MOTEL

Taking advantage of the golfer's interest in Blowing Rock, the **Greenview Motel** advertised "US 321S. Altitude 4,000 feet, adjoins highest golf course east of the Rockies." This motel has been razed and was replaced by the Fairway Villas Condominiums, which enjoy an incredible view of the golf course.

The Ridgeway Motel *was not shy about touting itself as "one of Blowing Rock's finest, located in the Heart of Town, where 221 meets 321." This conveniently located motel is now operated as Ridgeway Inn, and continues to provide for easy ambling about the village.*

Most of Blowing Rock's motels catered to the summer traveling guest. The **Parkway Motel** *was one of few that advertised that it was "open year 'round and had 10 modern units and 10 baths." This motel has been expanded and is now named Alpen Acres Motel. It is located just north of Blowing Rock on US 221/321.*

The Pine Court mentions a long famous Main Street restaurant in its advertising: "located on Blue Ridge Parkway and US Highways 221/321 one half block from the Wagon Wheel Grill - center of town - quiet location." This motel was owned by John Gaumer, and is now converted into the Shops of Watership Down. Its location just off Main Street made it accessible to all the village offered.

The Village Motel boasted it was "quiet and close in, just below the Post Office" when it was on Sunset Drive (before the new post office was built in 1976 in its current location on North Main Street below First Union Bank). The motel is now named the Alpine Village Inn.

The **Azalea Garden Motel** has long been known for its beautiful grounds and gardens. It was a pacesetter in establishing the garden traditions that make Blowing Rock especially beautiful in the warmer months. Owned by Mr. and Mrs. Jack Rainey for many years, the motel now is known as The Azalea Garden Inn.

Known for its "clear view for 50 miles", the **Valley View Motel** also touted its location "60 feet from The Rock and 1/2 mile from Blowing Rock." Located on the old Lenoir-Blowing Rock Turnpike (US 321) the motel is currently being converted into studio condominiums called Village Gate.

A more recent view of the **Blowing Rock Motor Court**, located on Morris Street.
Ultra-modern for its day, it was owned by Mr. and Mrs. Omer Coffey. It has been demolished.

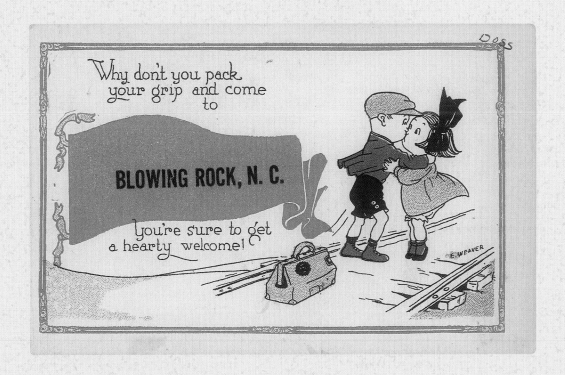

Blowing Rock has long been touted as North Carolina's finest tourist

destination. Many come for its fine restaurants and great food!

The Chestnut Restaurant *announced on the back of its card: "Fine Food, US 321-221 No. Main Street." This restaurant, once named Buchanan's, is now known as Knights on Main. Note that the front door has been moved to the left side of the building. The interior is paneled with wormy chestnut wood.*

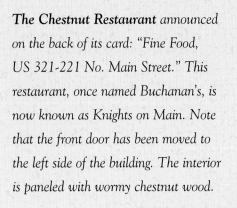

The Ranch Motel and Restaurant
was located close to the Blue Ridge Parkway and offered patrons convenience to both the scenic drive and the Village. The post card on the left shows the interior of the Ranch Restaurant. Navelli's Restaurant is now in this location just off US 321.

Mom & Pop's, located on Sunset Drive across from First Baptist Church, was opened as The Carriage House, a family restaurant. It is now the Village Pharmacy.

Blowing Rock's Main Street looking south shows one of downtown's favorite places to dine in the 1940's. **The Parkway Hotel**, *located across from the old Holshouser home and adjacent to the original first Baptist church, was a favorite dining spot for both local residents and visitors.*

StreetScene-Blowing Rock, N.C.   1-B-96

SUNSHINE INN, BLOWING ROCK, N. C.

STEAM HEAT   OPEN YEAR ROUND   ALTITUDE 4090 FEET

The Sunshine Inn, *located on Sunset Drive, owned and operated by the Burns family for many years, served family-style meals. Rates were quoted as "Room Single $1.00, Room with Meal $1.25" (this must have been around the early 1940's). Today it is Crippen's Country Inn and Restaurant.*

Mayview Manor Hotel *advertised "4800 feet high in the Blue Ridge Mountains: Mayview Manor is just off the Blue Ridge Parkway. Every comfort and recreational facility for a wonderful vacation 'above the clouds'." This is a view of the lovely chestnut paneled dining room. Mayview Manor was demolished in 1978, and has been replaced by the Mayview Manor Condominiums.*

The Chuck Wagon Restaurant
*specialized in country ham,
choice western steaks and
homemade biscuits in the 1960's.
The ABC Store is now housed in
this building on Valley Boulevard.*

The Farm House Inn and Restaurant,
*begun in 1945, was known for its food,
music and view! Advertising on the back
of the card "The fabulous Farm House
Lodge and Dining Rooms overlooking the
Johns River Valley 'above and beyond
life's trivialities' -- singing waiters and
waitresses" told the story well. This was
a popular summer restaurant; its dining
room could seat 500 people. The
building was demolished in 1999.*

ATTRACTIONS

Since before the incorporation of the Town of Blowing Rock in 1889, folks came to the area to escape the heat of the lowlands. As the popularity of Blowing Rock and The High Country grew, transportation became easier and many "attractions" and industries began to develop, all welcoming travelers to this area.

762 CAMP-LIFE IN THE MOUNTAINS

5A-H479

Camp life in the mountains seems to have supplied most of the comforts of home in the rugged outdoors. Much of the camping-out was necessary, as prior to the 1880's, hotels were few in Blowing Rock.

524:—CAMP LIFE IN THE HEART OF THE MOUNTAINS.

This is the **Shulls Mill Logging Camp** near what is now Hound Ears Resort. The Whiting Lumber Company and others in the industry provided an economic boost for the area at the turn of the century. The timber around Blowing Rock was logged and taken to the camp for milling, then loaded onto the Eastern Tennessee & Western North Carolina (ET&WNC - later called "Tweetsie") train to Johnson City, Tennessee.

This card shows **"Camp Life"** the way real mountain folks did it. While camping in the wilderness, one might as well make a little "moonshine" to sell to the city folks. They called it "moonshine" because it was most often made at night.

N-278 "TWEETSIE". FAMOUS EXCURSION TRAIN ON E. T. & W. N. C. RAILWAY

E-4461

A SCENE NEAR BOONE, N. C.

"Tweetsie", as the train became known for her "tweet" whistle, worked her way through the mountains from Johnson City, Tennessee to Boone, North Carolina. The narrow gauge railroad was officially the East Tennessee and Western North Carolina Railroad.

*In the early 1920's **Tweetsie** was mainly used for hauling freight and a few passengers, but as the popularity of the mountains grew, regular excursions were run through the mountains.*

RAILWAY TRAIN PULLING UP THE MOUNTAIN. "IN THE HEART OF THE BLUE RIDGE MOUNTAINS."

Building the track through the rough terrain was no easy task, as this post card shows. Sadly, the 1940 flood washed out so much of the track that **Tweetsie** was put out of service.

In the early 50's, **Tweetsie** was sold to be used in Hollywood films. The Robbins family decided the little train could be a great attraction for the area, and brought Tweetsie home to be enjoyed by generations to come.

This is a great post card from the 1940's showing the L. M. Tate Horse Show Grounds. While the emphasis was on horses, the **Blowing Rock Charity Horse Show** was also known as the major social event of the season. There were always many parties and gala events surrounding the annual Horse Show.

From this view of the grounds, one can see the fields that were used for the hunter and jumper classes. **The Blowing Rock Charity Horse Show** is the oldest continuous horse show in America, started in 1923, and still thriving today.

The Blowing Rock Charity Horse Show has continued to grow over the years. It began as an afternoon event, and now lasts for three weeks. This show attracts world class equestrians from all over the globe.

A number of summer camps enjoyed the mountain terrain and the healthy climate of the Blowing Rock area. The only post card available of the many camps in the area, is this one from **Camp Yonahlossee**, stating that it was a private camp for girls 7-16, and had provided "fun for girls since 1923". Dr. and Mrs. A.P. Kephart of Greensboro founded this innovative camping experience for girls and were widely praised for their success. The camp closed in the early 1980's, and the grounds are now part of The Yonahlossee Resort and Club on Shulls Mill Road.

Mystery Hill is another attraction close to Blowing Rock. This early card shows the museum before the first of two fires destroyed much of the attraction. As you can see in the top card, the fire didn't bother the old hillbilly 'cause he's still kicking at a location near Tweetsie.

Preservation has always been an important part of exhibits at **Mystery Hill**, as shown by this post card of old-timey mountain tools and household items. Today, Mystery Hill also offers tours of the old Dougherty House.

The Mountain Shop, *located on the Linville Highway (US 221) was opened and was operated for many years by Daisy and Rom Adams. It is now The Village Hardware.*

In 1950 John Goodwin brought a 175-year old tradition of colonial weaving, combined with seven generations of expertise, from Virginia to create **Goodwin Weavers** and the Blowing Rock Crafts Company.

A quote from John Goodwin on one card says: "You are invited to watch and inspect these artists bringing forth new creations." Goodwin Weavers sold the company a few years ago, but many local homes still proudly display bedspreads, placemats and other special pieces from their looms.

83

Appalachian Ski Mountain was opened in 1962 as the Blowing Rock Ski Slope. These scenes show skiers taking lessons and waiting their turn to go down the slope.

Night skiing with a brilliant lighting system at Appalachian brought many fans their first opportunity to participate in the sport.

This card shows the second chairlift installed at **Appalachian Ski Mountain** in North Carolina's famous "Winter Sports Capital" at Blowing Rock.

Two "firsts" for **Appalachian Ski Mountain** are shown on this card: the first snowcat and the first airless snowmaking machine in the southeast.

BLOWING ROCK COUNTRY CLUB
AND GOLF COURSE

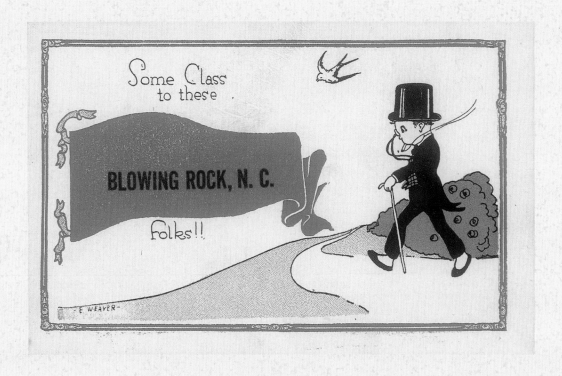

This "banner" or "pennant" card is from a series of Sentimental Kid cards (No. 2325) probably dating to the 1930's, made in the USA and printed with various towns' names. We thought it made a good introduction to special "top-hat" events at the Country Club.

N-750   GOLF COURSE ADJOINING GREEN PARK HOTEL, BLOWING ROCK, N. C., "IN THE LAND OF THE SKY"

E-7873

1939 marked the beginnings of the **Blowing Rock Country Club** when about 60 cottagers purchased six acres of land next to the Green Park-Norwood Golf Course. The completion of the rustic style, native stone country club was celebrated with a gala opening on July 4, 1941.

GOLF AND COUNTRY CLUB - BLOWING ROCK, N. C

The **Blowing Rock Country Club**, pictured here, served its members and guests as a haven from the worries of World War II and a social gathering spot for 33 years. Tragically, it was destroyed by fire on September 21, 1974.

N-622   COUNTRY CLUB, BLOWING ROCK, N. C.

E-5764

Photo by Emerson Humphrey

This 1965 aerial view card states: "This excellent view shows **Blowing Rock Country Club**, the highest elevation of any golf course in Eastern America, one of three Championship Courses in the Blowing Rock, Boone, NC area."

114:—Golfing on one of the Beautiful Courses, Blowing Rock, N. C. Grandfather Mt. in distance.

George Blagg, the Club's first pro, is photographed on the tee in the early 40's. Although the golf course remained under separate ownership, the golf shop was moved to the Club and the holes were numbered to allow play to begin and end at the golf shop. **The Country Club** bought the course in the early 1970's.

In 1913, the Blowing Rock Development Company purchased the Green Park Inn and 365 acres surrounding it to build a **nine-hole golf course**, which was completed in 1915. In 1922 the course was expanded to 18 holes under the guidance of golf course designer Donald Ross.

109:—Green Park Hotel as Seen from Golf Links, Green Park, N. C. near Blowing Rock.

Golfers enjoy the glorious view as well as cool temperatures at the "highest golf course in the United States, east of the Rockies, elevation 4300 feet." A Model T drives by on the Lenoir-Blowing Rock Turnpike, now US 321.

Greetings from

Blowing Rock, N. C.

Where the world is at its best.

1927

Travel to Blowing Rock was not always as easy as it is today. It is hard for modern travelers to relate to the perils of the late 19th century. These early cards show some of the difficulties that varying modes of transportation and road conditions presented to tourists coming to our lovely town almost a hundred years ago.

It would be hard to get folks to bring their goods to market on a sled, much less in a
"Sunday-go-to-meeting" hat. This hardworking lady shows the true pioneer spirit.
This post card is postmarked 1910.

The first automobile came to Blowing Rock in 1908, *and the style of travel began to change, as seen in these early cards.*

Old and New Way of Locomotion.
Blowing Rock, N. C.

In this "old and new way of locomotion", we wonder if the oxen or the auto got up the mountain first!

Leaning Rock
Yonahlossee
Linville, N. C.

Ten minutes to Boone, thirty minutes to Lenoir
or Linville was not always the way. These folks
seem to be ready for a picnic as the trip to
Linville was an all-day affair along the
Yonahlossee turnpike (now Highway 221) at
the time this card was in circulation (c. 1910).

This is the **road to Boone**, which
follows closely the current route of
US 321 North along the fork of
the New River.

On the Turnpike to Boone through the Valley
of the New River, Blowing Rock, N. C.

128:—Panoramic View Showing the Highway that Climbs Mountain on Way to Blowing Rock, N. C.

22241

This wonderful panoramic
view of the Lenoir-
Blowing Rock turnpike *has*
a note on the back stating:
"This is about 1/4 of the
way up, and the road isn't
half as wide as pictured."

N-747   BLOWING ROCK HIGHWAY, WITH GRANDFATHER MOUNTAIN IN DISTANCE, BLOWING ROCK, N. C.

This card from the
1950's shows US
321 and Grandfather
Mountain as seen
between Green Park
and the Town of
Blowing Rock.

E-7870

The Beautiful Blowing Rock Country.
Sunset Rock on Cliff Drive.
GREEN PARK, N. C.

There were so many great views from numerous spots along the road near Blowing Rock. This one was taken on **Cliff Drive** in the (then) Town of Green Park, N.C., which was annexed as part of Blowing Rock in 1927. Today, three private residences are built on this road.

The Beautiful Blowing Rock Country.
Blowing Rock, N. C.

Sunset Rock on Cliff Drive.

This card, dated September 1912, depicts Sunset Rock on **Cliff Drive**, located just off Pinnacle Avenue between downtown and Green Park. Cliff Drive still hugs the landscape overlooking the John's River Gorge, and hasn't changed much since this photograph was taken almost ninety years ago. (Note that the same card is used with different descriptions and borders.)

107:—Wonderland Trail Roadway, Mayview Park, Blowing Rock, N. C.

*This card of **Wonderland Trail** in the Mayview Park section shows the early construction technique of many of Blowing Rock's roads. Many were built with log foundations in the early 1920's.*

*One of the popular stops while touring around the area was the Nose End Rock on the **Trail of the Black Bear** (Yonalasee Road) opened in 1889.*

119:—Nose End Rock, on the Yonalasee Road, Blowing Rock Section, Western North Carolina.

430:—Scene on Black Bear Trail, between Blowing Rock and Boone, N. C.

117:—Scene from Blowing Rock Roadway, Western North Carolina.

396:—ROADWAY SCENE, "IN THE HEART OF THE MOUNTAINS."

*These early cards portray both how rugged and beautiful the **roads in the Blowing Rock** area were. It was truly an adventure to tour our mountain byways at the turn of the twentieth century!*

On the handwritten postcard:

My dear Margaret:— Louise, Pauline and I July 17—1904 are all ... writing letters and postals and of course I could not forget you. The postal you sent me from Atlantic City certainly was good of you and I appreciated it ever so much. I know you all have a good time at the Chelsea and wish you would all come up here now. ... much love to all of us.

On the Boone Road, near Blowing Rock, N.C.

Arthur Livingston, Publisher, New York. 636

Grandfather Mountain from Yonahlossee Road.
Blowing Rock, N. C.

The **road to Boone** wasn't always a super slab of concrete and asphalt. In 1904 it wound through the dense woodlands by a number of landmark boulders. Even the old road bed of this 18-mile route from Blowing Rock has been lost to history, replaced by a widened and improved roadway in the 1940's that put Blowing Rock only 11 miles from Boone. Today, the distance is about eight miles along a new corridor that carries traffic on a four-lane section of asphalt. This rare post card left room on both sides for the sender's message.

Yonahlossee Road was one of the earliest wagon ways built in the rugged mountains in the Blowing Rock area. Today we know it as Highway 221. The property that can be seen in this old card, looking out toward Grandfather Mountain, may have been a family home. Yonahlossee, like Watauga, Appalachian, and Catawba, are all words from the Cherokee language, and are the only reminders that this land was once the proud home of the many native of Americans.

GRANDFATHER MOUNTAIN

From the 1940's onward, Grandfather Mountain has grown from an inaccessible, primitive area to one of North Carolina's most visited natural attractions. "Grandfather" has always been one of the most scenic and special vistas from Blowing Rock as well as offering exceptional views from its famous "mile high swinging bridge".

At one time, the only approach to Grandfather Mountain was the old Indian Trail. Now, however, it is easily accessible through the mountains' highway system as well as the Blue Ridge Parkway.

In 1935 an abandoned roadway built in the 1890's was improved and extended to the first peak of the mountain. It was later upgraded again for the opening of the **"mile high swinging bridge"** in September 1952 by the mountain's owner, Hugh Morton.

950:— OBSERVATION POINT AND TOP OF GRANDFATHER MOUNTAIN. WESTERN NORTH CAROLINA.

This may have been the first observation tower at **Grandfather**, built in 1936. A cabin was built by the Linville Improvement Company, whose founder, Hugh MacRae, wanted to promote the attractions of the area.

112:—Grandfather Mountain from Yonalasee Road near Linville, N. C.

This excellent view of **Grandfather Mountain** *is looking across MacRae Meadows from the old Yonalasee (now spelled Yonahlossee) Road.*

Perspective of Grandfather. Blowing Rock, N. C.

Views of **Grandfather** *from Blowing Rock were as popular with the tourists at the turn of the twentieth century as they are now.*

BLOWING ROCK, N. C.

The Grandfather Mountain, from the Turnpike Road.
20 miles distant.   Elevation 5897 feet.

Grandfather Mt. from Green's Hill.   Blowing Rock, N. C.

Coming up the old Lenoir-
Blowing Rock Turnpike (now US
321) provided some extraordinary
views of **Grandfather Mountain**.
This card is postmarked 1916.

Grandfather Mountain as seen
from Green's Hill, named after
Blowing Rock's first family. The "s"
in Green's was dropped in later
years. This is a hand-colored Earl
Hardy photograph, circa 1930.

586:—Grandfather Mountain as seen from Blowing Rock, Western North Carolina.

1936

This is a beautiful view from The Blowing Rock, across the John's River gorge to **Grandfather Mountain**, dated August 8, 1936.

Winter scenes of **Grandfather Mountain** with snowcapped peaks offer some of the most spectacular views.

178—"Singing on the Mountain", Grandfather Mountain, N. C.

© CURT TEICH & CO., INC.

7B-H1749

In 1926 Joe Hartley began Grandfather's **"Singing on the Mountain"** as a family gathering that grew and grew. It is still as popular now as it was when this colortone card was produced in the 1930's.

The **Highland Games** have become one of the largest Scottish clan gatherings not only in the United States, but the entire world. The event, always held the second weekend in July, was started in 1956 to celebrate the contributions of the Scots to our heritage, and to keep alive the Scottish traditions in America. This card was photographed by Hugh Morton.

Waterfalls were so spectacular to "flatlanders" that families packed into new
horseless carriages to view them and other wonders of mountain scenery.

GLEN MARIA FALLS
NEAR BLOWING ROCK. N.C.

7918

Glen Maria Falls *is probably one of Blowing Rock's best kept secrets. Cascading over ancient boulders into the John's River Gorge, Glen Maria (today more familiarly known as "Glen Marie Falls") has been a favorite with hikers since the turn of the century. Few people know that the land through which Glen Marie and the Glen Burnie Falls flows was deeded to the Town of Blowing Rock in the 1940's with the stipulation that it always remain a park open to the public.*

Near Blowing Rock, N. C.

"SILVER VALE FALLS"   View by the way-side en-Route to Blowing Rock, N. C.   Bradshaw   Hickory, N. C

©1934

In the early days, postal cards of these beautiful landscapes were among the most popular with vacationers wanting to share their mountaintop adventure with their friends from back home.

Silver Vale Falls *and a number of other classic mountain waterfalls rambling from the rugged cliffs leading to Grandfather Mountain made for a photographer's paradise.*

308—Highway between Lenoir and Blowing Rock, N. C. showing Water Falls

2A81-N

Nothing sets the atmosphere of a perfect mountain landscape more than a waterfall splashing its way through the tall timbers and boulders of a hillside. In the early days of Blowing Rock's development as a tourism destination, roadways were built miles out of their way to simply pass a picturesque waterfall or mountain stream. The old road leading to the village from Lenoir was one of those roadways, and along **Highway 221** waterfalls are evident all the way from Blowing Rock to Linville.

No.1 GLEN BURNIA FALLS NEAR BLOWING ROCK, N.C.

Glen Burnie has been a rich part of Blowing Rock's history since the village was incorporated in 1889. Long before then, however, the trail passing this most famous of all Blowing Rock waterfalls was a popular spot for picnicking, hiking or getting close to nature. The Glen Burnie, once considered too dangerous for the town to promote as a park, is now listed as a more strenuous hike limited to those only fit enough to test the steep trails.

"GLEN BURNIE" NEAR BLOWING ROCK, N.C.

Arthur Livingston, Publisher, New York. 634

Leading from South Main Street all the way down the John's River Gorge, **Glen Burnie** is more of a cascade than a falls, leaving the distinction of being a true waterfall to Glen Marie, just a few hundred feet above Glen Burnie.

One interesting fact about this particular waterfall is its name, publicized as Glen Burney, Glen Burnie, and even Glen Burnia. The different views in these old postal cards are from the early 1900s when Glen Burnie was a favorite destination for those looking for the rugged beauty surrounding the Village of Blowing Rock.

GLEN BURNIE, NEAR BLOWING ROCK, N. C.

317—Glen Burney Falls in Glen Burney Park

Blowing Rock, N. C., Alt. 4,000 Ft.

Twin Falls near Blowing Rock.

PUB. FOR GREEN PARK HOTEL

America's Switzerland. The unrivaled Blowing Rock Country. Twin Falls near Blowing Rock, N.C.

The description of Blowing Rock as "America's Switzerland" appears again in these old post cards of **"Twin Falls"** near Blowing Rock.

A family is pictured enjoying a series of smaller waterfalls that dot the landscape along Highway 221. The date on this card was October 8, 1908.

Here is **Bridal Veil Falls**, located on Yonahlossee Road near Blowing Rock.

Bridal Veil Falls on Yonahlossee Road. Blowing Rock, N. C.

„Land of the Sky" Blowing Rock, N. C.

Visitors to Blowing Rock had a hard time sharing by word of mouth the beauty of the **Blue Ridge Mountains**, and for that reason, a picture was worth a thousand words. Post cards which depict scenes like this mountain view were common in the 1920's and gave many travelers a memento of their visit to the mountains.

The mountains around Blowing Rock are truly sights to behold. Since its founding as a traveler's destination in the early and mid-1800's, the Blowing Rock area has offered its visitors far more than a distant view of the lowlands. A **mountain stream** in the Blowing Rock country was also something to brag about for visitors as well as locals.

A Mountain Stream in the Blowing Rock Country.
Blowing Rock, N. C.

A typical mountain scene showing **Flat Top Mountain** in the background was a favorite with visitors to Blowing Rock in 1918. But who wouldn't be impressed with such a wonderful sight as mountain cabins nestled amid a backdrop of beautiful woodlands and distant mountain peaks?

102:—Scene showing Flat Top Mt., Blowing Rock, N. C. "In the Land of the Sky."

Above the Clouds in the Beautiful Blowing Rock Country, "The Switzerland of America."
BLOWING ROCK, N.C.
Altitude 4300 feet.

While the slogan on this old post card calls Blowing Rock "The Switzerland of America", a more fitting description might be **"Cloudland"** for indeed that is the view from a village located above the clouds in this post card circa 1916.

126:—View from Green's Hill, Blowing Rock, N. C. Showing Clouds over Grandfather Mt.

1932

The view from Green's Hill looking across at **Grandfather Mountain** showed only the faintest handprint of man on the landscape. Today, some 100 years since this old post card was in circulation, the same view has more signs of development between the village and Grandfather's profile. Known today simply as Green Hill, it is one of Blowing Rock's most attractive residential neighborhoods.

One of the luxuries of living on top of a mountain is the privilege of **seeing a storm forming** and moving across the distant hills, through valleys, and up to the mountaintop Village of Blowing Rock. That pleasure hasn't lessened since man first set foot in our area, as depicted in this post card circa 1912.

Looking off Blowing Rock, Storm in the distance.   BLOWING ROCK, N. C.

Wooded Mountains of Western North Carolina.
Near Blowing Rock, N. C.

Silverglo
BRISTOL, VA.
3. R 9

The **view from the top of the mountain** offers residents and
visitors alike one of the most impressive sights in the world. In this
card, the photographer captured a scene of unspoiled mountains as
they were back then. Today these mountains are dotted with
developments and other visible signs of man's impact on the region.

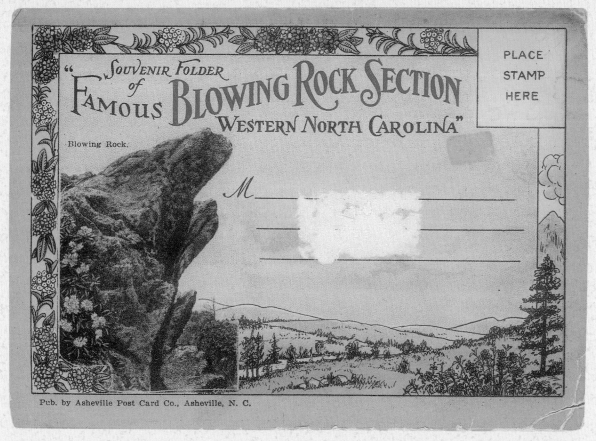

Souvenir folders of multiple views were introduced in the 1930's, providing many pictures of an area for a small price, with little room for a message and a bit more postage required for mailing. The folder cards became mini-scrapbooks that were saved as mementos of one's travels at a time when cameras were not common to most vacationers. The fold-out card usually enveloped in a heavier paper folder contained nine views on each side of the fold, for a total of eighteen. Inside that packet was a long descriptive narrative telling of the attractions, climate, scenery, and recreation facilities of the Blowing Rock area. The back of the folder provides another space for special views or drawings to enhance the images.

The nine "fold-overs" shown here feature a montage of pictures of The Rock, Grandfather Mountain, crafts, flora, scenery, bears and deer, cloud formations, the Blue Ridge Parkway and other mountain roadways praising the auto accessibility of the area. Many of the folders announced fishing and golfing as the most popular forms of recreation in the 1940's. The glorious mountain views and enticing narratives provided a grand marketing tool for bringing visitors to this bucolic area of the Blue Ridge Mountains. These folders became a collectible souvenir for those who wanted to share with others their vacation experience in the Blowing Rock area.

Scenes along
BLUE RIDGE
PARKWAY

GREETINGS FROM
BLOWING
and BOO

Daddy
Souvenir FOLDER of
The LAND OF THE SKY

SPRINGTIME

POSTAGE
1½ c
WITHOUT
MESSAGE

BLOW

Master John David Wray
510 Dixie trail
Raleigh, N.C.

120

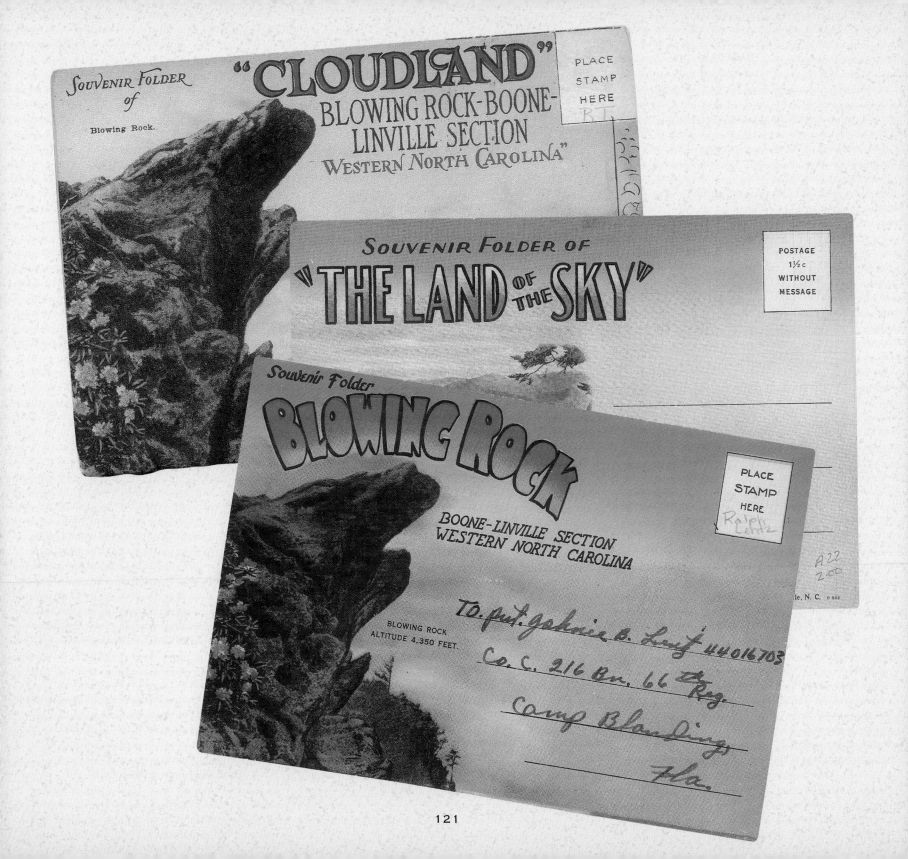

As post cards became a statement of vacation venues, and an opportunity to share with friends and family special views the writer enjoyed, different types of cards were developed. Miniature post cards were done of some places, but none was found for Blowing Rock.

However, GIANT cards (5 1/2 x 8 3/4 inches) produced in the 1960's celebrated some of the most picturesque vistas of our town's namesake. These two cards had more room for correspondence and required extra postage, but really made a BIG impression on the receiver.

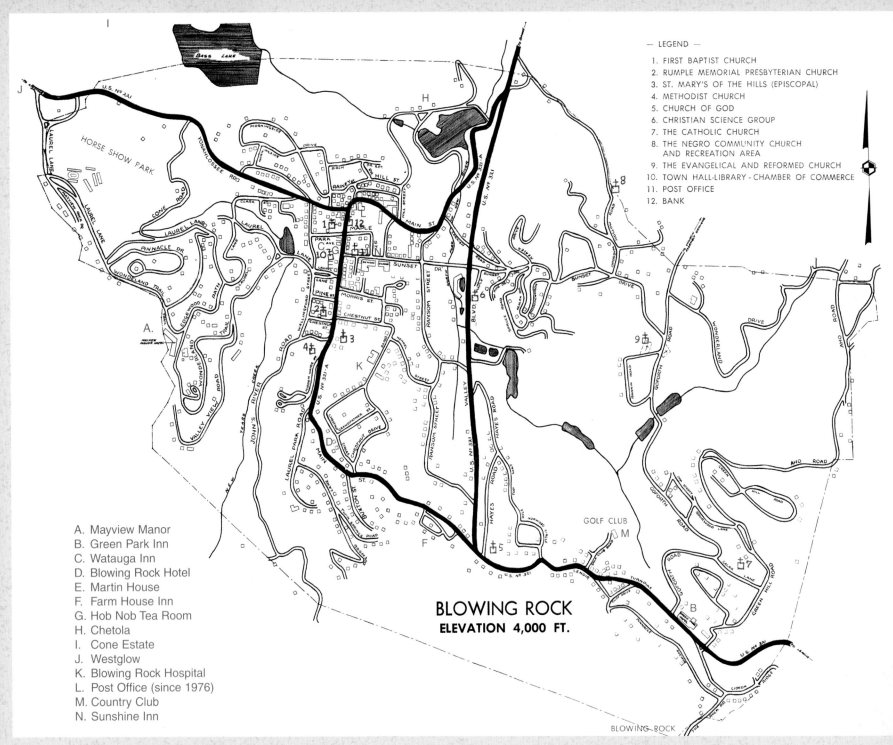

— LEGEND —

1. FIRST BAPTIST CHURCH
2. RUMPLE MEMORIAL PRESBYTERIAN CHURCH
3. ST. MARY'S OF THE HILLS (EPISCOPAL)
4. METHODIST CHURCH
5. CHURCH OF GOD
6. CHRISTIAN SCIENCE GROUP
7. THE CATHOLIC CHURCH
8. THE NEGRO COMMUNITY CHURCH
   AND RECREATION AREA
9. THE EVANGELICAL AND REFORMED CHURCH
10. TOWN HALL-LIBRARY - CHAMBER OF COMMERCE
11. POST OFFICE
12. BANK

A. Mayview Manor
B. Green Park Inn
C. Watauga Inn
D. Blowing Rock Hotel
E. Martin House
F. Farm House Inn
G. Hob Nob Tea Room
H. Chetola
I. Cone Estate
J. Westglow
K. Blowing Rock Hospital
L. Post Office (since 1976)
M. Country Club
N. Sunshine Inn

BLOWING ROCK
ELEVATION 4,000 FT.

This map, used by the Chamber of Commerce in the 1960's, has been modified to show additional landmarks which are in red.

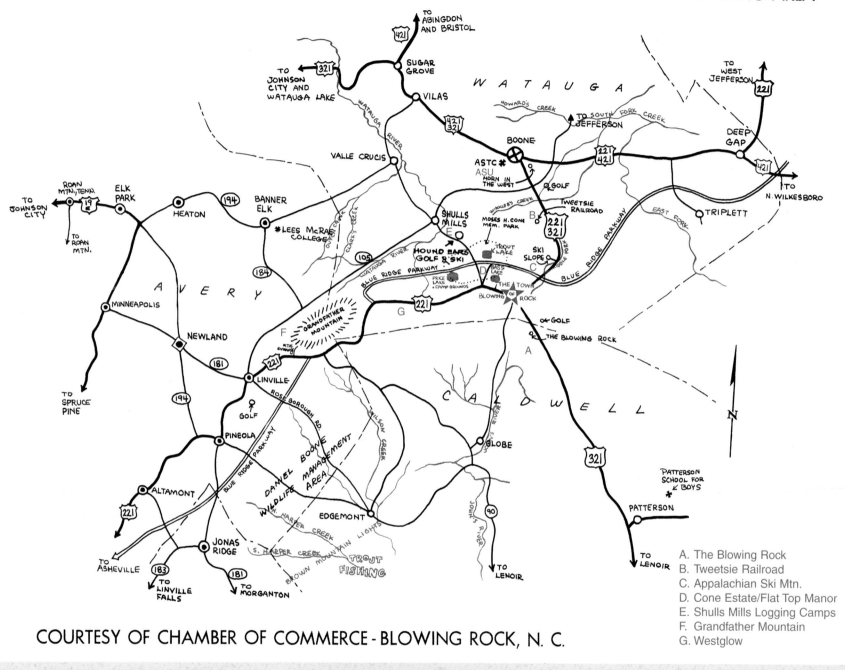

POINTS OF INTEREST
IN BLOWING ROCK AND SURROUNDING AREA

TO ABINGDON AND BRISTOL

421

TO JOHNSON CITY AND WATAUGA LAKE

321

SUGAR GROVE

VILAS

WATAUGA

HOWARD'S CREEK

TO SOUTH FORK CREEK
JEFFERSON

TO WEST JEFFERSON

221

DEEP GAP

421
321

BOONE

221
421

421
TO N. WILKESBORO

VALLE CRUCIS

WATAUGA RIVER

ASTC
ASU
HORN IN THE WEST

GOLF

TRIPLETT

ROAN MTN., TENN.
ELK PARK

19

TO JOHNSON CITY

TO ROAN MTN.

194

BANNER ELK

HEATON

LEES McRAE COLLEGE

CLARK'S CREEK
OLD FIELD CREEK

SHULLS MILLS
E

MOSES H. CONE MEM. PARK

WINKLER'S CREEK

Tweetsie Railroad

B

221
321

EAST FORK

MINNEAPOLIS

AVERY

184

105

WATAUGA RIVER

HOUND EARS GOLF & SKI

TROUT LAKE

SKI SLOPE
C

MIDDLE FORK

BLUE RIDGE PARKWAY

NEWLAND

F

GRANDFATHER MOUNTAIN

MTN. SWINGS

BLUE RIDGE PARKWAY

PRICE LAKE & CAMP GROUNDS

BASS LAKE
D

THE TOWN OF BLOWING ROCK

G

221

GOLF

THE BLOWING ROCK

A

181

221

LINVILLE

ROSE BOROUGH RD.

194

GOLF

TO SPRUCE PINE

WILSON CREEK

JOHN'S RIVER

GLOBE

321

PINEOLA

BLUE RIDGE PARKWAY

DANIEL BOONE WILDLIFE MANAGEMENT AREA

PATTERSON SCHOOL FOR BOYS

PATTERSON

N

ALTAMONT

221

N. HARPER CREEK

S. HARPER CREEK

BROWN MOUNTAIN LIGHTS

TROUT FISHING

EDGEMONT

JOHN'S RIVER

90

TO LENOIR

TO LENOIR

JONAS RIDGE

TO ASHEVILLE

183

TO LINVILLE FALLS

181

TO MORGANTON

A. The Blowing Rock
B. Tweetsie Railroad
C. Appalachian Ski Mtn.
D. Cone Estate/Flat Top Manor
E. Shulls Mills Logging Camps
F. Grandfather Mountain
G. Westglow

COURTESY OF CHAMBER OF COMMERCE - BLOWING ROCK, N. C.

Please note that ASTC is Appalachian State Teachers College, now Appalachian State University (ASU).